PANSIES

PANSIES

Introduction by
Scott D. Appell

MetroBooks

MetroBooks

An Imprint of Friedman/Fairfax Publishers

Library of Congress Cataloging-in-Publication Data available upon request.

ISBN 1-58663-064-4

Editor: Sharyn Rosart
Art Director: Jeff Batzli
Designer: Milagros Sensat
Production Manager: Karen Matsu Greenberg

Color separations by Colourscan Co. Pte. Ltd.
Printed in China by Leefung-Asco Printers

1 3 5 7 9 10 8 6 4 2

For bulk purchases and special sales, please contact:
Friedman/Fairfax Publishers
Attention: Sales Department
15 West 26th Street
New York, NY 10010
212/685-6610 FAX 212/685-1307

Visit our website:
www.metrobooks.com

These little [pansies] have infinite variety of expression; some

are laughing and roguish, some sharp and shrewd, some sur-

prised, others worried...a few are saucy to a degree, [but] all

are animated and vivacious.

—Alice Morse Earle, 1901

Pansies in a bouquet, convey the message of thoughts.

—Kate Greenaway, c. 1865

Many gardeners have fond memories of pansies dating back to our childhood recollections of gardens. Peeping up from the early spring garden, their beaming "faces" made an indelible impression. Of course, the pansy is not the only plant that lingers in memory—we may recall with equal delight our first encounter with gigantic sunflowers, our first whiff of pungent tomato foliage, and our earliest taste of freshly-picked sun-warmed raspberries. But the pansy alone stands out as the only flower to smile back at us.

Pansies are available in a disarming array of color combinations. Add to that their light sweet scent, their ease of culture, and their inclination to bloom throughout mild winters, and it is easy to understand why pansies are among the most widely used and cherished of garden flowers in North America and Europe alike.

You may be surprised to discover that the modern garden pansy does not exist in the wild.

Most of our familiar garden subjects (trees, shrubs, perennials, and annuals) were derived from the careful selection and propagation of wild plants. However, the garden pansy as we know it today was intentionally developed by gardeners who hybridized several European wildflowers to create a genetic base. Indeed, the pansy did not even exist until the 1820s, and it never grew in American soil until just prior to the Civil War. Ironically, the parental history of this charmingly simple flower is incredibly complex—and steeped in mythology, folklore, religion, and magic.

The modern garden pansy belongs to the plant family Violaceae, the violets. They typically have five petals, four of which are arranged in pairs, with each pair differing. The genus *Viola* encompasses about 500 species, including the garden pansy, viola, violetta, and violet. Botanically, the garden pansy is known as *Viola × wittrockiana*. Taxonomically, the "×" in the scientific name automatically tells us that the plant is the hybrid offspring of different species parents—either naturally occurring or human-induced. At the turn of the century, the pansy was alternately known as *Viola tricolor maxima* and *V. t. hortensis*.

The modern garden pansy was bred and selected in Victorian England during the 1820s through '40s by a horticulturist named Thompson, who was the head gardener for British naval commander Lord Gambier. Thompson worked on hybridizing *Viola tricolor* (what we know as the Johnny-jump-up), a native of Europe, Asia, and the Baltic region, with *V. lutea* subsp. *sudetica* (the yellow-flowered Hudson Mountain pansy), which is indigenous to western and central Europe. Botanists speculate whether he incorporated a third species into the mix—*V. altaica* (the Altai Mountain pansy), native to the Crimea and Altai Mountains. By mid-century, there were more than 400 cultivars available.

Today, pansy flowers are divided into two categories—fancy and show. Varieties of the latter are further sub-divided, according to the color of their flowers, into three classes: white grounds, yellow grounds, and selfs. Selfs may be black, maroon, primrose, white, or yellow, with petals that may be blotched, flamed or edged.

The common name "pansy" has two probable derivations. One is from the French word *pensée*, meaning thought or remembrance. The other may be a corruption of "pain's ease," an allusion to the medicinal properties of *Viola tricolor*. In fact,

Johnny-jump-ups are mildly diuretic, and help to cleanse the system and stimulate the metabolism. Herbalists also prescribe them for skin diseases and rheumatism.

Historically, the diminutive *V. tricolor* was most beloved as an ingredient of love philtres or potions. The ancient Celts used the dried flowers and leaves in a decoction. Folklore has it that at one time all pansies were pure white, and it was not until pierced by Cupid's arrow that the flowers

bloomed purple and yellow as well. William Shakespeare (after reading accounts of the flower in the Renaissance herbals of John Gerard[e] in 1587) referred to the pansy as "before milk-white, now purple with love's wound, And maidens call it love-in-idleness." He was well aware (as was all of Tudor England) of the pansy's magic, especially in inducing love. In A *Midsummer-Night's Dream*, Oberon instructs Puck in its use on Titania:

> *The juice of it, on sleeping eye-lids laid,*
> *Will make a man or woman madly dote*
> *Upon the next live creature that it sees.*

The spurned Ophelia specifies "And there is pansies, that's for thoughts," as she gives away flowers during her mad scene in Hamlet.

A plethora of love-related common names arose between the Middle Ages and Jacobean era, including heartsease, kitty-come, cuddle-me, ladies'-delight, love-in-idleness, cull-me-to-you, tickle-my-fancy, kiss-her-in-the-pantry and the astonishing meet-her-in-the-entry-kiss-her-in-the-buttery—which must be longest common name we have in English. The inimitable Victorian horti-culturist Gertrude Jekyll referred to the pansy with

the remarkable epithet of welcome-home-husband-be-he-ever-so-drunk (incidentally, she never married).

It is the black markings and petal arrangement of the Johnny-jump-up that have given the modern garden pansy its "face." The pansy's smiling visage has elicited scores of common names, including monkey face, kit-run-about, peeping Tom, and three faces in the hood.

Garden pansies began to wane in popularity between the two World Wars—mostly because they were so labor intensive to propagate. (Pansies don't breed true from seed and have to be increased manually by cuttings.) During this time many of the older cultivars were lost completely. However, there are some heirloom varieties still available, including the bronze and yellow 'Jackanapes' (named after Gertrude Jekyll's pet monkey), which dates from about 1890, and the award-winning, pale lavender and primrose 'Maggie Mott', which was introduced prior to 1902.

Today, garden pansies are again enormously popular. Breeders are developing countless new cultivars annually, and varieties are bountiful, so that every pansy taste can be satisfied. If the flowers with the familiar black blotches no longer please, there are a number of new pastel selfs to try—the tangerine 'Jolly Joker', pale-yellow 'Clear Sky Primrose,' and silver-pink 'Sterling Silver', for example. Formerly, garden pansies would dwindle and succumb to summer's warmth, but now there are heat-resistant varieties, including 'Water Colours Mixed,' 'Frosty Rose,' and 'Velour Clear Blue'.

In areas with mild winters, sow packaged (not collected or saved) seed or set out plants in early autumn for hibernal blooms. Where summers are hot, sow seed indoors during January or February, and set out young plants in early spring. All pansies prefer a rich loamy soil and plenty of moisture. Picking small bouquets, nosegays, or tussie-mussies will keep them in flower.

The flowers and foliage of pansies are edible—and surprisingly high in vitamins C and A. The lightly fragrant blossoms have a faint lettuce-like taste. Although previously pansy flowers were reserved strictly as salad decoration, our "horto-culinary" expertise is expanding. We now bake them onto cookies and affix them to ganache-covered cakes with glimmering drops of royal icing. Creative cooks encase them within shimmering layers of white wine aspic onto cold poached chicken breasts, salmon fillets, or pale wheels of

brie or camembert. Party hosts may freeze them in ice to add a decorative chill to beverages, and what sweeter treat could a gardener want but a candied pansy?

—Scott D. Appell

Bibliography

Asimov, Isaac. *Asimov's Guide to Shakespeare*. Wings Books, New York. 1970.

Bayard, Tanya. *A Medieval Home Companion*. HarperPerennial, New York. 1991.

Brewster, Kate L. *The Little Garden for Little Money*. The Atlantic Monthly Press, Boston. 1924.

Brickell, Christopher. *The American Horticultural Society Encyclopedia of Garden Plants*. Macmillan Publishing Co., New York. 1992.

Caotorta, Francesca Marzotto. *Sapore di Viole e Mille e una Panse*. Elle Decore (Italiano) 1997.

Cavallo, Adolfo Salvatore. *The Unicorn Tapestries at the Metropolitan Museum of Art*. Harry N. Abrams, Inc., Publishers, New York. 1998.

Conway, Amy. *Pansies and Violas*. Martha Stewart Living Magazine. May 1998.

Earle, Alice Morse. *Old-Time Gardens*. MacMillan & Co., New York. 1901.

Greenaway, Kate. *The Language of Flowers*. Gramercy Publishing Company, New York. 1884.

Griffiths, Mark. RHS *Index of Garden Plants*. Timber Press, Portland, Oregon. 1994.

Laroque, Francois. *Shakespeare: Court, Crowd and Playhouse*. Thames and Hudson, London. No date.

The Metropolitan Museum of Art. *The Unicorn Tapestries*. Privately published. 1974.

Nicholson, George, editor. *The Illustrated Dictionary of Gardening*. L. Upcott Gill, London. 1900.

O'Conner, Evangeline M., *Who's Who and What's What in Shakespeare*. Crown Publishers, New York. 1978.

Phillips, Roger and Foy, Nicky. *The Random House Book of Herbs*. Random House, New York. 1990.

Phillips, Roger and Rix, Martin. *The Random House Book of Perennials (Vol. 1)* Random House, New York. 1991.

Polunin, Oleg. *A Field Guide to Wildflowers of Europe*. Oxford University Press, London & New York. 1969.

Roberts, Mark. *Putting on the Charm*. Gardens Illustrated Magazine. John Brown Publishing Ltd. 1997.

Tankard, Judith B. And Wood, Martin A. *Gertrude Jekyll at Munstead Wood*. Sagapress, Inc. 1996.

Photography Credits